POPE BENEDICT XVI

FAMILY

Spiritual Thoughts Series

Introduction by Lucio Coco

D0932288

United States Conference of Catholic Bishops
Washington, D.C.

OTHER TITLES IN THE SPIRITUAL THOUGHTS SERIES

Spiritual Thoughts in the First Year of His Papacy
St. Paul
Mary
The Saints
The Word of God

First printing, June 2009

ISBN: 978-1-60137-075-4

CONTENTS

he family is the privileged setting where every person learns to give and receive love.

—POPE BENEDICT XVI

INTRODUCTION

Leafing through the pages of this small book, which is a collection of some of Pope Benedict XVI's thoughts on the subject of family, it is lovely to reflect with the Holy Father on the truth of marriage, which is the expression of God's plan for man and woman to become one flesh (see Gn 2:24), and on the theological basis of this union: God who is love created man for love. The vocation of love is therefore what makes man the authentic image of God, as Benedict took the opportunity to say in a brilliant passage from one of his speeches: "man and woman come to resemble God to the extent that they become loving people" (Address, June 6, 2005).

The unique and definitive quality of marriage is rooted in this bond of love existing between God and man: God's way of loving becomes the measure of human love, so that "corresponding to the image of a monotheistic God is monogamous marriage" (*Deus Caritas Est*, no. 11). Its indissolubility is also a quality that is intrinsic to the nature of this "powerful bond established by the Creator" (Pope John Paul II, Audience, November 21, 1979). It is true that this original design, which includes God's plan for man and constitutes his inner purpose, may be clouded and threatened today by cultures that tend to belittle, disregard, and relativize the principle of this union. But Pope Benedict XVI has affirmed—responding to the questions of young people on the occasion of the meeting in preparation for the Twenty-First World Youth Day—that "man was never able to forget completely this plan that exists in the depths of his being. He has always known, in a certain sense, that other forms of relationship between a man and a woman do not truly correspond with the original design for his being. And thus, in cultures, especially in the great cultures, we see again and again how they are oriented to this reality: monogamy, the man and the woman becoming one flesh" (Address, April 6, 2006).

Uniqueness and definitiveness: it is here that the truth and beauty of marriage is found. But how can this be understood? The Holy Father asks, "How it is possible to communicate the beauty of marriage to the people of today?" (Address, August 31, 2006). This is the problem of a "joyful and anguished" time (*Urbi et Orbi*, December 25, 2006)—of our time, where any choice, any decision, or any commitment is put off or avoided in the name of a mistaken understanding of freedom as being the individual's only source of moral law, as being "a fundamental value to which all others must be subject" (Address, October 19, 2006). Pope Benedict has frequently repeated that this freedom, which claims the right to do whatever it desires, in this case detaches itself from the good of the husband, wife, and children (see Address, August 31, 2006), is arbitrary (see Address, February 10, 2006), and is a pseudo-freedom leading not to liberation but to a serious form of dependence and slavery: "so often," the Pope writes, "freedom is presented as a relentless search for pleasure or new experiences. Yet this is a condemnation not a liberation!" (Message, January 24, 2007). In this way, such freedom falls into licentiousness and sets itself against the dignity of the person (see Address, June 6, 2005). Pope Benedict explains that true freedom is not about merely having fun, or considering oneself completely autonomous, "but rather about living by the measure of truth and goodness" (Homily, August 21, 2005). Freedom is found in the "yes" of a commitment, like the promises of spouses and the *fiat* of Mary, "the perfect disciple of her Son, who realizes the fullness of his freedom and thus exercises freedom through obedience to the Father" (Homily, March 25, 2006).

The family bonds that the Holy Father discusses are strong ones, intended to guard against any ambiguity and any drifting toward weak or partial solutions, which would end up denaturing the essence of marriage. Non-negotiable principles for any family policies include the "recognition and promotion of the natural structure of the family—as a union between a man and a woman based on marriage—and its defense from attempts to make it juridically equivalent to radically different forms of union which in reality harm it and contribute to its destabilization, obscuring its particular character and its irreplaceable social role" (Address, March 30, 2006). The Church has the task of protecting and guaranteeing these principles, since her concern and primary care are for humanity and human dignity, and her duty is to defend this "human being, that creature who, precisely in the inseparable unity of body and spirit, is the image of God" (Address, December 22, 2006).

After attempting to increase our awareness by recalling the weaknesses afflicting families today—where relationships are often fleeting, parents are missing, and sound intergenerational communication is lacking—at the same time Pope Benedict wishes to provide us with a good model. With this aim, he never tires of describing the family as "the first and principal place where life is welcomed" (Address, December 30, 2005), of insisting on the positive outlook on life—"despite all difficulties" (Address, July 8, 2006)—that parents must transmit to their children, and of insisting on the relational dimension of the family as an open space where children "learn" to live (see Homily, July 9, 2006). The family must be built, and it acquires its unique shape and identity precisely through crises, losses, and suffering, as Benedict XVI sought to emphasize in reflecting on his trip to Valencia (July 8-9, 2006): "thus, from the witness of these families a wave of joy reached us, not a superficial and scant gaiety that is all too soon dispelled, but a joy that developed also in suffering, a joy that reaches down to the depths and truly redeems man" (Address, December 22, 2006).

The Holy Father invites us to undertake an extraordinary quest—as he himself makes clear—"for the meaning of the human being" (Address, December 22, 2006). This invitation is extended through his desire for us to reflect on the thoughts he offers regarding family: the family as the sanctuary of love, life, and faith—as the domestic Church, but also as a school of culture and humanity, where children learn to use their intellect, to choose freely, to place themselves in the service of love, and to understand the good and importance of prayer, through which new vocations may flourish. Following these indications from Pope Benedict's teachings, along the path of the doctrines and teachings of the Church (see Address, June 6, 2005), one finds it possible to build and develop a Gospel of the family—understood as a journey of human and spiritual fulfillment—in which love can mature "to be fully human and the principle of a true and lasting joy" (Address, July 8, 2006). Pope Benedict XVI invites us to work and commit ourselves to success in this endeavor, with the assurance that throughout history and in the lives of our families "the Lord is always present with his grace" (Address, December 3, 2005).

Lucio Coco

FAMILY

1. *Goal*

I wish to set forth the central role, for the Church and for society, proper to the family based on marriage. The family is a unique institution in God's plan, and the Church cannot fail to proclaim and promote its fundamental importance, so that it can live out its vocation with a constant sense of responsibility and joy.

Welcome ceremony at Manises Airport, Valencia, Spain
July 8, 2006

I. THE TRUTH OF MARRIAGE

2. *The biblical account of marriage*

The first novelty of biblical faith consists, as we have seen, in its image of God. The second, essentially connected to this, is found in the image of man. The biblical account of creation speaks of the solitude of Adam, the first man, and God's decision to give him a helper. Of all other creatures, not one is capable of being the helper that man needs, even though he has assigned a name to all the wild beasts and birds and thus made them fully a part of his life. So God forms woman from the rib of man. Now Adam finds the helper that he needed: "This at last is bone of my bones and flesh of my flesh" (Gn 2:23). Here one might detect hints of ideas that are also found, for example, in the myth mentioned by Plato, according to which man was originally spherical, because he was complete in himself and self-sufficient. But as a punishment for pride, he was split in two by Zeus, so that now he longs for his other half, striving with all his being to possess it and thus regain his integrity. While the biblical narrative does not speak of punishment, the idea is certainly present that man is somehow incomplete, driven by nature to seek in another the part that can make him whole, the idea that only in communion with the opposite sex can he become "complete." The biblical account thus concludes with a prophecy about Adam: "Therefore a man leaves his father and his mother and cleaves to his wife and they become one flesh" (Gn 2:24). Two aspects of this are important. First, *eros* is somehow rooted in man's very nature; Adam is a seeker, who "abandons his mother and father" in order to find woman; only together do the two represent complete humanity and become "one flesh." The second aspect is equally important. From the standpoint of creation, *eros* directs man towards marriage, to a bond which is unique and definitive; thus, and only thus, does it fulfill its deepest purpose. Corresponding to the image of a monotheistic God is monogamous marriage. Marriage based on exclusive and definitive love becomes the icon of the relationship between God and his people and vice versa. God's way of loving becomes the measure of human love. This close connection between *eros* and marriage in the Bible has practically no equivalent in extra-biblical literature.

Encyclical Letter God Is Love (Deus Caritas Est), *no. 11*
December 25, 2005

3. *The theological basis for marriage*

Marriage and the family are not in fact a chance socio-logical construction, the product of particular historical and financial situations. On the other hand, the question of the right relationship between the man and the woman is rooted in the essential core of the human being, and it is only by starting from here that its response can be found. In other words, it cannot be separated from the ancient but ever new human question: Who am I? What is a human being? And this question, in turn, cannot be separated from the question about God: Does God exist? Who is God? What is his face truly like? The Bible gives one consequential answer to these two queries: the human being is created in the image of God, and God himself is love. It is therefore the vocation to love that makes the human person an authentic image of God: man and woman come to resemble God to the extent that they become loving people.

This fundamental connection between God and the person gives rise to another: the indissoluble connection between spirit and body: in fact, the human being is a soul that finds expression in a body, and a body that is enlivened by an immortal spirit. The body, therefore, both male and female, also has, as it were, a theological character: it is not merely a body; and what is biological in the human being is not merely biological but is the expression and the fulfillment of our humanity. Likewise, human sexuality is not juxtaposed to our being as person but part of it. Only when sexuality is integrated within the person does it successfully acquire meaning.

Address to participants in the ecclesial diocesan convention of Rome June 6, 2005

4. *The basis for marriage in the natural law*

The natural law, together with fundamental rights, is the source from which ethical imperatives also flow, which it is only right to honor. In today's ethics and philosophy of Law, petitions of juridical positivism are widespread. As a result, legislation often becomes only a compromise between different interests: seeking to transform private interests or wishes into laws that conflict with the duties deriving from social responsibility. In this situation it is opportune to recall that every juridical methodology, be it on the local or international level, ultimately draws its legitimacy from its rooting in the natural law, in the ethical message inscribed in the actual human being. Natural law is, definitively, the only valid bulwark against the arbitrary power or the deception of ideological manipulation. The knowledge of this law inscribed on the heart of man increases with the progress of the moral conscience. The first duty for all, and particularly for those with public responsibility, must therefore be to promote the maturation of the moral conscience. This is the fundamental progress without which all other progress proves non-authentic. The law inscribed in our nature is the true guarantee offered to everyone in order to be able to live in freedom and to be respected in their own dignity. What has been said up to this point has very concrete applications if one refers to the family, that is, to "the intimate partnership of life and the love which constitutes the married state . . . established by the Creator and endowed by him with its own proper laws" (*Gaudium et Spes*, no. 48). Concerning this, the Second Vatican Council has opportunely recalled that the institution of marriage has been "confirmed by the divine law," and therefore "this sacred bond . . . for the good of the partner, of the children and of society no longer depends on human decision alone" (*Gaudium et Spes*, no. 48). Therefore, no law made by man can override the norm written by the Creator without society's becoming dramatically wounded in what constitutes its basic foundation. To forget this would mean to weaken the family, penalizing the children and rendering the future of society precarious.

> *Address to participants in the International*
> *Congress on Natural Moral Law*
> *February 12, 2007*

5. *Marriage in salvation history*

The truth about marriage and the family, deeply rooted in the truth about the human being, has been actuated in the history of salvation, at whose heart lie the words: "God loves his people." The biblical revelation, in fact, is first and foremost the expression of a history of love, the history of God's Covenant with humankind. Consequently, God could take the history of love and of the union of a man and a woman in the covenant of marriage as a symbol of salvation history. The inexpressible fact, the mystery of God's love for men and women, receives its linguistic form from the vocabulary of marriage and the family, both positive and negative: indeed, God's drawing close to his people is presented in the language of spousal love, whereas Israel's infidelity, its idolatry, is designated as adultery and prostitution. In the New Testament God radicalizes his love to the point that he himself becomes, in his Son, flesh of our flesh, a true man. In this way, God's union with humankind acquired its supreme, irreversible form. Thus, the blueprint of human love is also definitely set out, that reciprocal "yes" which cannot be revoked: it does not alienate men and women but sets them free from the different forms of alienation in history in order to restore them to the truth of creation. The sacramental quality that marriage assumes in Christ, therefore, means that the gift of creation has been raised to the grace of redemption. Christ's grace is not an external addition to human nature, it does not do violence to men and women but sets them free and restores them, precisely by raising them above their own limitations. And just as the Incarnation of the Son of God reveals its true meaning in the Cross, so genuine human love is self-giving and cannot exist if it seeks to detach itself from the Cross.

Address to participants in the ecclesial
diocesan convention of Rome
June 6, 2005

6. *The Sacrament of Marriage*

Marriage . . . as a natural institution is a "patrimony of humanity." Moreover, its elevation to the loftiest dignity of a sacrament must be seen with gratitude and wonder, as I recently said, affirming: "The sacramental quality that marriage assumes in Christ therefore means that the gift of creation has been raised to the grace of redemption. Christ's grace is not an external addition to human nature, it does not do violence to men and women but sets them free and restores them, precisely by raising them above their own limitations" (Address to the ecclesial diocesan convention of Rome, June 6, 2005).

Address at a meeting on family and
life issues in Latin America
December 3, 2005

7. *God's plan for man and woman*

For me it is a beautiful thing to observe that already in the first pages of Sacred Scripture, subsequent to the story of man's Creation, we immediately find the definition of love and marriage. The sacred author tells us: "A man will leave his father and mother and will cleave to his wife, and they will become one flesh," one life (Gn 2:24-25). We are at the beginning and we are already given a prophecy of what marriage is; and this definition also remains identical in the New Testament. Marriage is this following of the other in love, thus becoming one existence, one flesh, therefore inseparable; a new life . . . is born from this communion of love that unites and thus also creates the future. Medieval theologians, interpreting this affirmation which is found at the beginning of Sacred Scripture, said that marriage is the first of the seven sacraments to have been instituted by God already at the moment of creation, in Paradise, at the beginning of history and before any human history. It is a sacrament of the Creator of the universe, hence, it is engraved in the human being himself, who is oriented to this journey on which man leaves his parents and is united to a woman in order to form only one flesh, so that the two may be a single existence. Thus, the sacrament of marriage is not an invention of the Church; it is really "con-created" with man as such, as a fruit of the dynamism of love in which the man and the woman find themselves and thus also find the Creator who called them to love. It is true that man fell and was expelled from Paradise; or, in other words, more modern words, it is true that all cultures are polluted by the sin, the errors of human beings in their history, and that the initial plan engraved in our nature is thereby clouded. Indeed, in human cultures we find this clouding of God's original plan. At the same time, however, if we look at cultures, the whole cultural history of humanity, we note that man was never able to forget completely this plan that exists in the depths of his being. He has always known, in a certain sense, that other forms of relationship between a man and a woman do not truly correspond with the original design for his being. And thus, in cultures, especially in the great cultures, we see again and again how they are oriented to this reality: monogamy, the man and the woman becoming one flesh. This is how a new generation can grow in fidelity, how a cultural tradition can endure, renew itself in continuity and make authentic progress.

Encounter with youth in Lazio, Rome, before the
Twenty-First World Youth Day
April 6, 2006

8. *"And the two of them become one body" (Gn 2:24)*

Marriage and the family are rooted in the inmost nucleus of the truth about man and his destiny. Sacred Scripture reveals that the vocation to love is part of the authentic image of God which the Creator has desired to impress upon his creature, calling them to resemble him precisely to the extent in which they are open to love. Consequently, the sexual difference that distinguishes the male from the female body is not a mere biological factor but has a far deeper significance. It expresses that form of love with which man and woman, by becoming one flesh, as Sacred Scripture says, can achieve an authentic communion of people [who are] open to the transmission of life and who thus cooperate with God in the procreation of new human beings.

Address to members of the John Paul II
Institute on Marriage and the Family
May 11, 2006

9. *"Uni-duality"*

In *Mulieris Dignitatem*, John Paul II wished to deepen the fundamental anthropological truths of man and woman, the equality of their dignity and the unity of both, the well-rooted and profound diversity between the masculine and the feminine and their vocation to reciprocity and complementarity, to collaboration and to communion (cf. no. 6). This "uni-duality" of man and woman is based on the foundation of the dignity of every person created in the image and likeness of God: . . . "male and female he created them" (Gn 1:27), avoiding an indistinct uniformity and a dull and impoverishing equality as much as an irreconcilable and conflictual difference (cf. John Paul II, *Letter to Women*, no. 8). This dual unity brings with it, inscribed in body and soul, the relationship with the other, love for the other, interpersonal communion that implies "that the creation of man is also marked by a certain likeness to the divine communion" (*Mulieris Dignitatem*, no. 7). Therefore, when men and women demand to be autonomous and totally self-sufficient, they run the risk of being closed in a self-reliance that considers ignoring every natural, social or religious bond as an expression of freedom, but which, in fact, reduces them to an oppressive solitude. To promote and sustain the real advancement of women and men one cannot fail to take this reality into account.

Address to participants in the convention on the theme "Woman and Man: The Humanum *in Its Entirety" February 9, 2008*

10. *The importance of communion*

"God, who is love and who created man and woman for love, has called them to love. By creating man and woman he called them to an intimate communion of life and love in Marriage. 'So they are no longer two but one flesh' (Mt 19:6)" (*Compendium of the Catechism of the Catholic Church*, no. 337). This is the truth that the Church tirelessly proclaims to the world. My beloved predecessor Pope John Paul II said that "man has been made 'in the image and likeness of God' not only by his being human, but also by the communion of the persons that man and woman have formed since the beginning. They become the image of God, not so much in their aloneness as in their communion" (Catechesis, November 14, 1979).

> *Address at prayer vigil for the*
> *Fifth World Meeting of Families*
> *July 8, 2006*

11. *The beauty of marriage*

How is it possible to communicate the beauty of marriage to the people of today? We see how many young people are reluctant to marry in church because they are afraid of finality; indeed, they are even reluctant to have a civil wedding. Today, to many young people and even to some who are not so young, definitiveness appears as a constriction, a limitation of freedom. And what they want first of all is freedom. They are afraid that in the end they might not succeed. They see so many failed marriages. They fear that this juridical form, as they understand it, will be an external weight that will extinguish love.

It is essential to understand that it is not a question of a juridical bond, a burden imposed with marriage. On the contrary, depth and beauty lie precisely in finality. Only in this way can love mature to its full beauty. But how is it possible to communicate this? I think this problem is common to us all.

Meeting with priests of the Diocese of Albano
August 31, 2006

12. *The service of love*

Marriage is a Sacrament for the salvation of others: first of all for the salvation of the other, of the husband and of the wife, but also of the children, the sons and daughters, and lastly of the entire community.

Meeting with priests of the Diocese of Albano
August 31, 2006

13. *God's plan*

To those who asked him whether it was lawful for a man to divorce his wife, as provided by a decree in Mosaic law (cf. Dt 24:1), [he answered] that this was a concession made to Moses because of man's "hardness of heart," whereas the truth about marriage dated back to "the beginning of creation" when, as is written of God in the Book of Genesis, "male and female he created them; for this reason a man shall leave his father and mother and be joined to his wife, and the two shall become one" (Mk 10:6-7; cf. Gn 1:27; 2:24). And Jesus added: "So they are no longer two but one. What therefore God has joined together, let no man put asunder" (Mk 10:8-9). This is God's original plan, as the Second Vatican Council also recalled in the Constitution *Gaudium et Spes*: "The intimate partnership of life and love which constitutes the married state has been established by the Creator and endowed by him with its own proper laws: it is rooted in the contract of its partners. . . . God himself is the author of marriage" (no. 48).

Angelus
October 8, 2006

14. *The indissolubility of marriage*

"What therefore God has joined together, let no man put asunder" (Mt 19:6). Every marriage is of course the result of the free consent of the man and the woman, but in practice their freedom expresses the natural capacity inherent in their masculinity and femininity. The union takes place by virtue of the very plan of God who created them male and female and gives them the power to unite for ever those natural and complementary dimensions of their persons. The indissolubility of marriage does not derive from the definitive commitment of those who contract it but is intrinsic in the nature of the "powerful bond established by the Creator" (John Paul II, General Audience, November 21, 1979). People who contract marriage must be definitively committed to it because marriage is such in the plan of creation and of redemption. And the essential juridical character of marriage is inherent precisely in this bond which represents for the man and for the woman a requirement of justice and love from which, for their good and for the good of all, they may not withdraw without contradicting what God himself has wrought within them.

Address to members of the tribunal of the Roman Rota
January 27, 2007

15. *The juridical anthropology of marriage*

With regard to the subjective and libertarian relativization of the sexual experience, the Church's tradition clearly affirms the natural juridical character of marriage, that is, the fact that it belongs by nature to the context of justice in interpersonal relations. In this perspective, the law is truly interwoven with life and love as one of the intrinsic obligations of its existence. Therefore, as I wrote in my first Encyclical, "From the standpoint of creation, *eros* directs man towards marriage, to a bond which is unique and definitive; thus, and only thus, does it fulfill its deepest purpose" (*Deus Caritas Est*, no. 11). Thus, love and law can be united to the point of ensuring that husband and wife *mutually owe to one another* the love *with which they spontaneously love one another*: the love in them is the fruit of their free desire for the good of one another and of their children, which, moreover, is also a requirement of love for one's own true good.

Address to members of the tribunal of the Roman Rota
January 27, 2007

16. *The mission of marriage*

In the Apostolic Exhortation *Familiaris Consortio*, the Servant of God John Paul II wrote that "the sacrament of marriage makes Christian couples and parents witnesses of Christ 'to the end of the earth,' missionaries, in the true and proper sense, of love and life" (no. 54). Their mission is directed both to inside the family—especially in reciprocal service and the education of the children—and to outside it. Indeed, the domestic community is called to be a sign of God's love for all. The Christian family can only fulfill this mission if it is supported by divine grace. It is therefore necessary for Christian couples to pray tirelessly and to persevere in their daily efforts to maintain the commitments they assumed on their wedding day. I invoke upon all families, especially those in difficulty, the motherly protection of Our Lady and of her husband Joseph. Mary, Queen of the family, pray for us!

Angelus
October 8, 2006

II. THE FAMILY

17. *Forming a family*

[Dear young people,] above all, have great respect for the institution of the sacrament of Matrimony. There cannot be true domestic happiness unless, at the same time, there is fidelity between spouses. Marriage is an institution of natural law, which has been raised by Christ to the dignity of a sacrament; it is a great gift that God has given to mankind: respect it and honor it. At the same time, God calls you to respect one another when you fall in love and become engaged, since conjugal life, reserved by divine ordinance to married couples, will bring happiness and peace only to the extent that you are able to build your future hopes upon chastity, both within and outside marriage. I repeat here to all of you that "*eros* tends to rise . . . towards the Divine, to lead us beyond ourselves; yet for this very reason it calls for a path of ascent, renunciation, purification and healing" (Encyclical Letter *Deus Caritas Est*, no. 5). To put it briefly, it requires a spirit of sacrifice and renunciation for the sake of a greater good, namely the love of God above all things. Seek to resist forcefully the snares of evil that are found in many contexts, driving you towards a dissolute and paradoxically empty life, causing you to lose the precious gift of your freedom and your true happiness. True love "increasingly seeks the happiness of the other, is concerned more and more with the beloved, bestows itself and wants to 'be there for' the other" (*Deus Caritas Est*, no. 7) and therefore will always grow in faithfulness, indissolubility and fruitfulness.

Meeting with youth in São Paulo, Brazil
May 10, 2007

18. *The engagement period*

The love of a man and woman is at the origin of the human family, and the couple formed by a man and a woman has its foundation in God's original plan (cf. Gn 2:18-25). Learning to love each other as a couple is a wonderful journey, yet it requires a demanding "apprenticeship." The period of engagement, very necessary in order to form a couple, is a time of expectation and preparation that needs to be lived in purity of gesture and words. It allows you to mature in love, in concern and in attention for each other; it helps you to practice self-control and to develop your respect for each other. These are the characteristics of true love that does not place emphasis on seeking its own satisfaction or its own welfare. In your prayer together, ask the Lord to watch over and increase your love and to purify it of all selfishness. Do not hesitate to respond generously to the Lord's call, for Christian matrimony is truly and wholly a vocation in the Church.

Message for the Twenty-Second World Youth Day
January 27, 2007

19. *The "yes" of the spouses*

The totality of the person includes the dimension of time, and the person's "yes" is a step beyond the present moment: in its wholeness, the "yes" means "always," it creates the space for faithfulness. Only in this space can faith develop, which provides a future and enables children, the fruit of love, to believe in human beings. . . . The freedom of the "yes," therefore, reveals itself to be freedom capable of assuming what is definitive: the greatest expression of freedom is not the search for pleasure without ever coming to a real decision. . . . The true expression of freedom is the capacity to choose a definitive gift in which freedom, in being given, is fully rediscovered. In practice, the personal and reciprocal "yes" of the man and the woman makes room for the future, for the authentic humanity of each of them. At the same time, it is an assent to the gift of a new life. Therefore, this personal "yes" must also be a publicly responsible "yes," with which the spouses take on the public responsibility of fidelity, also guaranteeing the future of the community. None of us, in fact, belongs exclusively to himself or herself: one and all are therefore called to take on in their inmost depths their own public responsibility. Marriage as an institution is thus not an undue interference of society or of authority. The external imposition of form on the most private reality of life is instead an intrinsic requirement of the covenant of conjugal love.

Address to participants in the ecclesial
diocesan convention of Rome
June 6, 2005

20. *The place where life is welcomed*

I would like to stress the fundamental vocation of the family to be the first and principal place where life is welcomed. The modern concept of family, partly in reaction to the past, gives great importance to conjugal love, emphasizing its subjective aspects of freedom of choice and feelings. On the other hand, people are finding it harder to perceive and understand the value of the call to collaborate with God in procreating human life. Besides, contemporary societies, despite being equipped with so many means, do not always succeed in facilitating the mission of parents, either on the level of spiritual and moral motivations or on that of practical living conditions. There is a great need, both from the cultural and the political and legislative viewpoints, to support the family.

Visit to St. Martha's Dispensary, Vatican City
December 30, 2005

21. *Generational communion*

Families . . . are the fundamental cell of every healthy society. Only in families, therefore, is it possible to create a communion of generations in which the memory of the past lives on in the present and is open to the future. Thus, life truly continues and progresses. Real progress is impossible without this continuity of life, and once again, it is impossible without the religious element. Without trust in God, without trust in Christ who in addition gives us the ability to believe and to live, the family cannot survive.

Meeting with members of the Roman clergy
March 2, 2006

22. *Patrimony of humanity*

The family, founded on marriage, is the "patrimony of humanity," a fundamental social institution; it is the vital cell and pillar of society, and this concerns believers and non-believers alike. It is a reality that all States must hold in the highest regard because, as John Paul II liked to repeat, "the future of humanity passes by way of the family" (*Familiaris Consortio*, no. 86).

Address to participants in the plenary assembly of
the Pontifical Council for the Family
May 13, 2006

23. *Loving exchange*

Human beings were created in the image and likeness of God for love, and that complete human fulfillment only comes about when we make a sincere gift of ourselves to others. The family is the privileged setting where every person learns to give and receive love.

Address at the prayer vigil for the Fifth
World Meeting of Families in Valencia, Spain
July 8, 2006

24. *The family cell*

The family is an intermediate institution between individuals and society, and nothing can completely take its place. The family is itself based primarily on a deep interpersonal relationship between husband and wife, sustained by affection and mutual understanding. To enable this, it receives abundant help from God in the sacrament of Matrimony, which brings with it a true vocation to holiness. Would that our children might experience more the harmony and affection between their parents, rather than disagreements and discord, since the love between father and mother is a source of great security for children and it teaches them the beauty of a faithful and lasting love.

Address at the prayer vigil for the Fifth
World Meeting of Families in Valencia, Spain
July 8, 2006

25. *The truth about the family*

The family is a necessary good for peoples, an indispensable foundation for society and a great and lifelong treasure for couples. It is a unique good for children, who are meant to be the fruit of the love, of the total and generous self-giving of their parents. To proclaim the whole truth about the family, based on marriage as *a domestic Church and a sanctuary of life*, is a great responsibility incumbent upon all.

> *Address at the prayer vigil for the Fifth*
> *World Meeting of Families in Valencia, Spain*
> *July 8, 2006*

26. *Parents as models*

Together with passing on the faith and the love of God, one of the greatest responsibilities of families is that of training free and responsible persons. For this reason the parents need gradually to give their children greater freedom, while remaining for some time the guardians of that freedom. If children see that their parents—and, more generally, all the adults around them—live life with joy and enthusiasm, despite all difficulties, they will themselves develop that profound "joy of life" which can help them to overcome wisely the inevitable obstacles and problems which are part of life. Furthermore, when families are not closed in on themselves, children come to learn that every person is worthy of love, and that there is a basic, universal brother-hood which embraces every human being.

Address at the prayer vigil for the Fifth
World Meeting of Families in Valencia, Spain
July 8, 2006

27. *Family roles*

The family is irreplaceable for the personal serenity it provides and for the upbringing of children. Mothers who wish to dedicate themselves fully to bringing up their children and to the service of their family must enjoy conditions that make this possible, and for this they have the right to count on the support of the State. In effect, the role of the mother is fundamental for the future of society.

The father, for his part, has the duty to be a true father, fulfilling his indispensable responsibility and cooperating in bringing up the children. The children, for their integral growth, have a right to be able to count on their father and mother, who take care of them and accompany them on their way towards the fullness of life. Consequently there has to be intense and vigorous pastoral care of families. Moreover, it is indispensable to promote authentic family policies corresponding to the rights of the family as an essential subject in society. The family constitutes part of the good of peoples and of the whole of humanity.

Address to the Fifth General Conference of the Bishops of
Latin America and the Caribbean in Aparecida, Brazil
May 13, 2007

28. *School of humanity*

The family is also a school which enables men and women to grow to the full measure of their humanity. The experience of being loved by their parents helps children to become aware of their dignity as children.

> *Address at the prayer vigil for the Fifth*
> *World Meeting of Families in Valencia, Spain*
> *July 8, 2006*

29. *The relational dimension of the family*

None of us gave ourselves life or singlehandedly learned how to live. All of us received from others both life itself and its basic truths, and we have been called to attain perfection in relationship and loving communion with others. The family, founded on indissoluble marriage between a man and a woman, is the expression of this relational, filial and communal aspect of life. It is the setting where men and women are enabled to be born with dignity, and to grow and develop in an integral manner.

> *Homily at Mass in Valencia, Spain*
> *July 9, 2006*

30. *Source of peace*

In a healthy family life we experience some of the fundamental elements of peace: justice and love between brothers and sisters, the role of authority expressed by parents, loving concern for the members who are weaker because of youth, sickness or old age, mutual help in the necessities of life, readiness to accept others and, if necessary, to forgive them. For this reason, the family is *the first and indispensable teacher of peace*.

> *Message for the World Day of Peace*
> *December 8, 2007*

31. *Family relationships*

A family lives in peace if all its members *submit to a common standard*: this is what prevents selfish individualism and brings individuals together, fostering their harmonious coexistence and giving direction to their work.

> *Message for the World Day of Peace*
> *December 8, 2007*

32. *The family tree*

For me, in Valencia . . . it was an important moment . . . when various families presented themselves to me with one or more children; one family was virtually a "parish," it had so many children! The presence and witness of these families really was far stronger than any words. They presented first of all the riches of their family experience: how such a large family truly becomes a cultural treasure, an opportunity for the education of one and all, a possibility for making the various cultural expressions of today coexist, the gift of self, mutual help also in suffering, etc. But their testimony of the crises they had suffered was also significant. One of these couples had almost reached the point of divorcing. They explained that they then learned to live through this crisis, this suffering of the otherness of the other, and to accept each other anew. Precisely in overcoming the moment of crisis, the desire to separate, a new dimension of love developed and opened the door to a new dimension of life, which nothing but tolerating the suffering of the crisis could reopen.

Meeting with priests of the Diocese of Albano
August 31, 2006

33. *Grandparents*

May grandparents return to being a living presence in the family, in the Church and in society. With regard to the family, may grandparents continue to be witnesses of unity, of values founded on fidelity and of a unique love that gives rise to faith and the joy of living. The so-called new models of the family and a spreading relativism have weakened these fundamental values of the family nucleus. The evils of our society—as you justly observed during your work—are in need of urgent remedies. In the face of the crisis of the family, might it not be possible to set out anew precisely from the presence and witness of these people—grandparents— whose values and projects are more resilient? Indeed, it is impossible to plan the future without referring to a past full of significant experiences and spiritual and moral reference points. Thinking of grandparents, of their testimony of love and fidelity to life, reminds us of the Biblical figures of Abraham and Sarah, of Elizabeth and Zechariah, of Joachim and Anne, as well as of the elderly Simeon and Anna and even Nicodemus: they all remind us that at every age the Lord asks each one for the contribution of his or her own talents.

> *Address to participants in the plenary assembly of*
> *the Pontifical Council for the Family*
> *April 5, 2008*

34. *The celebrations of the family*

Family celebrations seem to me to be very important. On the occasion of celebrations it is right that the family, the beauty of families, appear.

> *Meeting with priests of the Diocese of Albano*
> *August 31, 2006*

35. *Memories from Valencia*

The visit to Valencia, Spain, was under the banner of the theme of marriage and the family. It was beautiful to listen, before the people assembled from all continents, to the testimonies of couples—blessed by a numerous throng of children—who introduced themselves to us and spoke of their respective journeys in the Sacrament of Marriage and in their large families. They did not hide the fact that they have also had difficult days, that they have had to pass through periods of crisis. Yet, precisely through the effort of supporting one another day by day, precisely through accepting one another ever anew in the crucible of daily trials, living and suffering to the full their initial "yes," precisely on this Gospel path of "losing oneself," they had matured, rediscovered themselves and become happy. Their "yes" to one another in the patience of the journey and in the strength of the Sacrament with which Christ had bound them together, had become a great "yes" to themselves, their children, to God the Creator and to the Redeemer, Jesus Christ. Thus, from the witness of these families a wave of joy reached us, not a superficial and scant gaiety that is all too soon dispelled, but a joy that developed also in suffering, a joy that reaches down to the depths and truly redeems man.

Christmas Address to the Roman Curia
December 22, 2006

36. *In defense of the identity of the family*

As Pastor of the universal Church, I cannot refrain from expressing to Your Excellency my anxiety for the laws that concern those very sensitive issues such as the transmission and defense of life, sickness, the identity of the family and respect for marriage. On these topics and in the light of natural reason and the moral and spiritual principles that derive from the Gospel, the Catholic Church will continue ceaselessly to proclaim the inalienable greatness of human dignity. It is also necessary to appeal to the responsibility of the lay people present in legislative bodies, in the Government and in the administration of justice to ensure that laws always express principles and values that are in conformity with natural law and that foster the authentic common good.

Address to the ambassador of Colombia to the Holy See
February 9, 2007

37. *Family policies (1)*

I invite government leaders and legislators to reflect on the evident benefits which homes in peace and harmony assure to individuals and the family, the neuralgic center of society, as the Holy See has stated in the *Charter of the Rights of the Family*. The purpose of laws is the integral good of man, in response to his needs and aspirations. This good is a significant help to society, of which it cannot be deprived, and for peoples a safeguard and a purification.

> *Address at the prayer vigil for the Fifth*
> *World Meeting of Families in Valencia, Spain*
> *July 8, 2006*

38. *Family policies (2)*

Special attention and extraordinary commitment are demanded today by those great challenges that endanger vast portions of the human family: war and terrorism, hunger and thirst, some terrible epidemics. But it is also necessary to face, with equal determination and clear policies, the risks of political and legislative choices that contradict fundamental values and anthropological principles and ethics rooted in the nature of the human being, in particular, regarding the guardianship of human life in all its stages, from conception to natural death, and to the promotion of the family founded on marriage, avoiding the introduction in the public order of other forms of union that would contribute to destabilizing it, obscuring its particular character and its irreplaceable role in society.

Address to participants in the Fourth
National Ecclesial Convention
October 19, 2006

39. *Family policies (3)*

This same concern for the human being that impels us to be close to the poor and the sick makes us attentive to that fundamental human good of the family based on marriage. Today, the intrinsic value and authentic motivations of marriage and the family need to be understood better. To this end, the Church's pastoral commitment has been considerable and must increase further. But a twofold policy of and for the family, which calls into question the responsibility of its members, is also necessary. In other words, it is a matter of increasing initiatives that can make the forming of a family and subsequently having and raising children easier and less burdensome for young couples; that encourage the employment of youth, contain housing costs as much as possible and increase the number of kindergartens and nursery schools. Indeed, those projects that aim to attribute to other forms of union inappropriate legal recognition inevitably lead to weakening and destabilizing the legitimate family founded on marriage.

Address to members of the administrations
of Rome and Lazio
January 11, 2007

40. *Needs of the family*

The family needs to have a home, employment and a just recognition of the domestic activity of parents, the possibility of schooling for children, and basic health care for all. When society and public policy are not committed to assisting the family in these areas, they deprive themselves of an essential resource in the service of peace.

Message for the World Day of Peace
December 8, 2007

41. *Peace of the family*

The peace of the family, then, requires an *openness to a transcendent patrimony of values*, and at the same time a concern for the prudent management of both material goods and interpersonal relationships. The failure of the latter results in the breakdown of reciprocal trust in the face of the uncertainty threatening the future of the nuclear family.

Message for the World Day of Peace
December 8, 2007

42. *Non-negotiable principles*

As far as the Catholic Church is concerned, the principal focus of her interventions in the public arena is the protection and promotion of the dignity of the person, and she is thereby consciously drawing particular attention to principles which are not negotiable. Among these the following emerge clearly today:

- protection of life in all its stages, from the first moment of conception until natural death;

- recognition and promotion of the natural structure of the family—as a union between a man and a woman based on marriage—and its defense from attempts to make it juridically equivalent to radically different forms of union which in reality harm it and contribute to its destabilization, obscuring its particular character and its irreplaceable social role;

- the protection of the right of parents to educate their children.

These principles are not truths of faith, even though they receive further light and confirmation from faith; they are inscribed in human nature itself, and therefore they are common to all humanity. The Church's action in promoting them is therefore not confessional in character, but is addressed to all people, prescinding from any religious affiliation they may have. On the contrary, such action is all the more necessary the more these principles are denied or misunderstood, because this constitutes an offence against the truth of the human person, a grave wound inflicted onto justice itself.

Address to members of the European People's Party
March 30, 2006

43. *Prayer for families*

The family . . . is the "cradle" of life and of every vocation. We are well aware that the family founded on marriage is the natural environment in which to bear and raise children and thereby guarantee the future of all of humanity. However, we also know that marriage is going through a deep crisis and today must face numerous challenges. It is consequently necessary to defend, help, safeguard and value it in its unrepeatable uniqueness. If this commitment is in the first place the duty of spouses, it is also a priority duty of the Church and of every public institution to support the family by means of pastoral and political initiatives that take into account the real needs of married couples, of the elderly and of the new generations. A peaceful family atmosphere, illumined by faith and the holy fear of God, also nurtures the budding and blossoming of vocations to the service of the Gospel. . . .

Dear brothers and sisters, let us pray that through a constant effort to promote life and the family institution, our communities may be places of communion and hope in which, despite the many difficulties, the great "yes" to authentic love and to the reality of the human being and the family is renewed in accordance with God's original plan.

Angelus
February 4, 2007

III. CHILDREN

44. *The begetting of children*

Even in the begetting of children marriage reflects its divine model, God's love for man. In man and woman, fatherhood and motherhood, like the body and like love, cannot be limited to the biological: life is entirely given only when, by birth, love and meaning are also given, which make it possible to say yes to this life. From this point it becomes clear how contrary to human love, to the profound vocation of the man and the woman, are the systematic closure of a union to the gift of life and even more, the suppression or manipulation of newborn life.

> *Address to participants in the ecclesial*
> *diocesan convention of Rome*
> *June 6, 2005*

45. *The right to life*

Children have the right to be born and to be raised in a family founded on marriage, where parents are the first educators of the faith for their children in order for them to reach full human and spiritual maturity. Children truly are the family's greatest treasure and most precious good. Consequently, everyone must be helped to become aware of the intrinsic evil of the crime of abortion. In attacking human life in its very first stages, it is also an aggression against society itself. Politicians and legislators, therefore, as servants of the common good, are duty-bound to defend the fundamental right to life, the fruit of God's love.

Address at a meeting on family and
life issues in Latin America
December 3, 2005

46. *Baptizing children*

Through Baptism each child is inserted into a gathering of friends who never abandon him in life or in death because these companions are God's family, which in itself bears the promise of eternity. This group of friends, this family of God, into which the child is now admitted, will always accompany him, even on days of suffering and in life's dark nights; it will give him consolation, comfort and light. This companionship, this family, will give him words of eternal life, words of light in response to the great challenges of life, and will point out to him the right path to take. This group will also offer the child consolation and comfort, and God's love when death is at hand, in the dark valley of death. It will give him friendship, it will give him life. And these totally trustworthy companions will never disappear. No one of us knows what will happen on our planet, on our European Continent, in the next fifty, sixty or seventy years. But we can be sure of one thing: God's family will always be present, and those who belong to this family will never be alone. They will always be able to fall back on the steadfast friendship of the One who is life.

> *Homily at Mass and celebration of*
> *Baptism in the Sistine Chapel*
> *January 8, 2006*

47. *An act of love*

A particularly sensitive topic today is the respect due to the human embryo, which ought always to be born from an act of love and should already be treated as a person (cf. *Evangelium Vitae*, no. 60). The progress of science and technology in the area of bioethics is transformed into a threat when human beings lose the sense of their own limitations and, in practice, claim to replace God the Creator. The Encyclical *Humanae Vitae* reasserts clearly that human procreation must always be the fruit of the conjugal act with its twofold unitive and procreative meaning (cf. no. 12). The greatness of conjugal love in accordance with the divine plan demands it, as I recalled in the Encyclical *Deus Caritas Est*: "*Eros* reduced to pure 'sex,' has become a commodity, a mere 'thing' to be bought and sold, or rather, man himself becomes a commodity. . . . Here we are actually dealing with a debasement of the human body" (no. 5). Thanks to God, many, especially young people, are rediscovering the value of chastity, which appears more and more as a reliable guarantee of authentic love.

Address to participants in the plenary assembly of the
Pontifical Council for the Family
May 13, 2006

48. *Generational continuity*

We see the threat to families; in the meantime even lay bodies recognize how important it is that the family live as the primary cell of society, that children be able to grow in an atmosphere of communion between the generations, so that continuity between the present, past and future will endure and that the continuity of values will be lasting: this is what makes it possible to build communion in a country.

Meeting with the German bishops around the Twentieth World Youth Day August 21, 2005

49. *Relationship and tradition*

Once children are born, through their relationship with their parents they begin to share in a family tradition with even older roots. Together with the gift of life, they receive a whole patrimony of experience. [In reference to this,] parents have the right and the inalienable duty to transmit this heritage to their children: to help them find their own identity, to initiate them to the life of society, to foster the responsible exercise of their moral freedom and their ability to love on the basis of their having been loved and, above all, to enable them to encounter God. Children experience human growth and maturity to the extent that they trustingly accept this heritage and training which they gradually make their own. They are thus enabled to make a personal synthesis between what has been passed on and what is new, a synthesis that every individual and generation is called to make.

Homily at Mass in Valencia, Spain July 9, 2006

50. *Divine filiation*

At the origin of every man and woman, and thus in all human fatherhood and motherhood, we find God the Creator. For this reason, married couples must accept the child born to them, not simply as theirs alone, but also as a child of God, loved for his or her own sake and called to be a son or daughter of God. What is more: each generation, all parenthood and every family has its origin in God, who is Father, Son and Holy Spirit.

Homily at Mass in Valencia, Spain
July 9, 2006

51. *Children's questions*

Where we come from, who we are, and how great is our dignity. Certainly we come from our parents and we are their children, but we also come from God, who has created us in his image and called us to be his children. Consequently, at the origin of every human being there is not something haphazard or chance, but a loving plan of God. This was revealed to us by Jesus Christ, the true Son of God and a perfect man. He knew whence he came and whence all of us have come: from the love of his Father and our Father.

Homily at Mass in Valencia, Spain
July 9, 2006

52. *Moral values for children*

What rules should we apply to ensure that the child follows the right path and in so doing, how should we respect his or her freedom? The problem has also become very difficult because we are no longer sure of the norms to transmit; because we no longer know what the correct use of freedom is, what is the correct way to live, what is morally correct and what instead is inadmissible. The modern spirit has lost its bearings, and this lack of bearings prevents us from being indicators of the right way to others. Indeed, the problem goes even deeper. Contemporary man is insecure about the future. Is it permissible to send someone into this uncertain future? In short, is it a good thing to be a person? This deep lack of self-assurance—plus the wish to have one's whole life for oneself—is perhaps the deepest reason why the risk of having children appears to many to be almost unsustainable. In fact, we can transmit life in a responsible way only if we are able to pass on something more than mere biological life, and that is, a meaning that prevails even in the crises of history to come and a certainty in the hope that is stronger than the clouds that obscure the future. Unless we learn anew the foundations of life—unless we discover in a new way the certainty of faith—it will be less and less possible for us to entrust to others the gift of life and the task of an unknown future. Connected with that, finally, is also the problem of definitive decisions: can man bind himself for ever? Can he say a "yes" for his whole life? Yes, he can. He was created for this. In this very way human freedom is brought about, and thus the sacred context of marriage is also created and enlarged, becoming a family and building the future.

Christmas Address to the Roman Curia
December 22, 2006

53. *Educating and witnessing*

I address you, dear parents, to ask you first of all to remain firm for ever in your reciprocal love: this is the first great gift your children need if they are to grow up serene, acquire self-confidence and thus learn to be capable in turn of authentic and generous love. Further, your love for your children must endow you with the style and courage of a true educator, with a consistent witness of life and the necessary firmness to temper the character of the new generations, helping them to distinguish clearly between good and evil so they in turn can form solid rules of life that will sustain them in future trials. Thus, you will enrich your children with the most valuable and lasting inheritance that consists in the example of a faith lived daily.

Presentation of a letter to the
Diocese of Rome on education
February 23, 2008

54. *The freedom of truth*

Neither parents nor priests nor catechists, nor any other educators can substitute for the freedom of the child, adolescent or young person whom they are addressing. The proposal of Christianity in particular challenges the very essence of freedom and calls it to faith and conversion. Today, a particularly insidious obstacle to the task of educating is the massive presence in our society and culture of that relativism which, recognizing nothing as definitive, leaves as the ultimate criterion only the self with its desires. And under the semblance of freedom it becomes a prison for each one. . . . With such a relativistic horizon, therefore, real education is not possible without the light of the truth; sooner or later, every person is in fact condemned to doubting in the goodness of his or her own life and the relationships of which it consists, the validity of his or her commitment to build with others something in common.

Address to participants in the ecclesial
diocesan convention of Rome
June 6, 2005

55. *Instilling the discernment of beauty*

Children exposed to what is aesthetically and morally excellent are helped to develop appreciation, prudence and the skills of discernment. Here it is important to recognize the fundamental value of parents' example and the benefits of introducing young people to children's classics in literature, to the fine arts and to uplifting music. While popular literature will always have its place in culture, the temptation to sensationalize should not be passively accepted in places of learning. Beauty, a kind of mirror of the divine, inspires and vivifies young hearts and minds, while ugliness and coarseness have a depressing impact on attitudes and behavior.

Message for the Forty-First World Communications Day
January 24, 2007

56. *The role of the media*

The social communications media, in particular, because of their educational potential, have a special responsibility for promoting respect for the family, making clear its expectations and rights, and presenting all its beauty.

Message for the World Day of Peace
December 8, 2007

57. *Relationship with communications media*

Like education in general, media education requires formation in the exercise of freedom. This is a demanding task.

So often freedom is presented as a relentless search for pleasure or new experiences. Yet this is a condemnation not a liberation! True freedom could never condemn the individual—especially a child—to an insatiable quest for novelty. In the light of truth, authentic freedom is experienced as a definitive response to God's "yes" to humanity, calling us to choose, not indiscriminately but deliberately, all that is good, true and beautiful. Parents, then, as the guardians of that freedom, while gradually giving their children greater freedom, introduce them to the profound joy of life.

Message for the Forty-First World Communications Day
January 24, 2007

58. *The media as an educational tool*

This heartfelt wish of parents and teachers to educate children in the ways of beauty, truth and goodness can be supported by the media industry only to the extent that it promotes fundamental human dignity, the true value of marriage and family life, and the positive achievements and goals of humanity. Thus, the need for the media to be committed to effective formation and ethical standards is viewed with particular interest and even urgency not only by parents and teachers but by all who have a sense of civic responsibility.

Message for the Forty-First World Communications Day
January 24, 2007

59. *Time for the children*

The problem of Europe, which it seems no longer wants to have children, penetrated my soul. To foreigners this Europe seems to be tired, indeed, it seems to be wishing to take its leave of history. Why are things like this? This is the great question. The answers are undoubtedly very complex. Before seeking these answers, it is only right to thank the many married couples in our Europe who still say "yes" to children today and accept the trials that this entails: social and financial problems, as well as worries and struggles, day after day; the dedication required to give children access to the path towards the future. In mentioning these difficulties, perhaps the reasons also become clearer why for many the risk of having children appears too great. A child needs loving attention. This means that we must give children some of our time, the time of our life. But precisely this "raw material" of life—time—seems to be ever scarcer. The time we have available barely suffices for our own lives; how could we surrender it, give it to someone else? To have time and to give time—this is for us a very concrete way to learn to give oneself, to lose oneself in order to find oneself.

Christmas Address to the Roman Curia
December 22, 2006

IV. THE FRAILTY OF THE FAMILY TODAY

60. *Historical background*

Christianity helped to shape European culture down the centuries. With the advent of Illuminism, Western culture began to drift more and more swiftly away from its Christian foundations. Especially in the most recent period, the break-up of the family and of marriage, attacks on human life and its dignity, the reduction of faith to a subjective experience and the consequent secularization of public awareness are seen as the stark and dramatic consequences of this distancing.

> *Address to media groups of the*
> *Italian bishops' conference*
> *June 2, 2006*

61. *The family in the current cultural context*

One crucial issue that demands of us the maximum pastoral attention is the family. In Italy, even more than in other countries, the family truly is the fundamental cell of society. It is deeply rooted in the hearts of the young generations and bears the brunt of many problems, providing support and remedies to situations that would otherwise be desperate. Yet also in Italy, families in today's cultural atmosphere are exposed to the many risks and threats with which we are all familiar. The inner frailty and instability of many conjugal unions is combined with the widespread social and cultural tendency to dispute the unique character and special mission of the family founded on marriage. Then, Italy itself is one of the nations where the low birth rate is the most serious and constant, with consequences that are already felt by the whole body of society. This is why . . . [we must defend] the sacredness of human life and the value of the institution of marriage, but also in promoting the role of the family in the Church and in society, requesting financial and legislative measures that support young families in having children and raising them.

> *Address to the fifty-fourth assembly of the*
> *Italian bishops' conference*
> *May 30, 2005*

62. *Dangers to the family*

Side by side with exemplary families, there are often others that are unfortunately marked by the frailty of conjugal bonds, the scourge of abortion and the demographic crisis, little attention to teaching authentic values to the children, the precariousness of employment, social mobility that weakens relations between the generations and a growing sense of inner bewilderment among the young people. A modernity that is not rooted in authentic human values is destined to be dominated by the tyranny of instability and confusion.

Address to bishops of Estonia, Latvia, and
Lithuania on their ad limina *visit*
June 23, 2006

63. *Families at risk*

The family institution deserves priority attention; it is showing signs of breaking up under the pressure of lobbies that can have a negative effect on legislative processes. Divorce and *de facto* unions are on the rise, while adultery is viewed with unjustifiable tolerance. It is necessary to reassert that marriage and the family are based on the deepest nucleus of the truth about man and his destiny; only on the rock of faithful and permanent conjugal love between a man and woman is it possible to build a community worthy of the human being.

Address to papal representatives of
Latin American countries
February 17, 2007

64. *Family instability*

In today's world, where certain erroneous concepts concerning the human being, freedom and love are spreading, we must never tire of presenting anew the truth about the family institution, as God has desired it since creation. Unfortunately, the number of separations and divorces is increasing. They destroy family unity and create numerous problems for children, the innocent victims of these situations. In our day it is especially the stability of the family that is at risk; to safeguard it one often has to swim against the tide of the prevalent culture, and this demands patience, effort, sacrifice and the ceaseless quest for mutual understanding. Today, however, it is possible for husbands and wives to overcome their difficulties and remain faithful to their vocation with recourse to God's support, with prayer and participating devotedly in the sacraments, especially the Eucharist. The unity and strength of families helps society to breathe the genuine human values and to be open to the Gospel.

> *Address to participants in the plenary assembly of*
> *the Pontifical Council for the Family*
> *May 13, 2006*

65. *Existential uncertainty*

Today, the order of marriage as established in creation and of which the Bible tells us expressly in the narrative of creation (cf. Gn 2:24) is gradually being obscured. To the extent that man seeks in new ways to build for himself the world as a whole, thereby ever more perceptibly endangering its foundations, he also loses his vision of the order of creation with regard to his own life. He considers he can define himself as he pleases by virtue of an inane freedom. Thus, the foundations that support his life and the life of society are undermined. It becomes difficult for young people to commit themselves definitively. They are afraid of finality, which seems to them impracticable and contrary to freedom. In this way it becomes more and more difficult to welcome children and to give them that lasting space for the growth and development that only the family founded on marriage can provide. In this situation just mentioned, it is very important to help young people say to themselves the definitive "yes" that is not in opposition to freedom but constitutes its greatest opportunity. Love reaches its true maturity in the patience required by being together for the whole of life. It is in this environment of lifelong love that children too must learn to live and love. Therefore, I would like to ask you to do all you can to see that marriage and the family are formed, promoted and encouraged.

> *Address to a group of German bishops*
> *on their* ad limina *visit*
> *November 18, 2006*

66. *Missing parents*

We can tangibly feel today . . . the problem of adolescents, their loneliness and their being misunderstood by adults. It is interesting that these young people who seek closeness in discotheques are actually suffering from great loneliness and, of course, also from misunderstanding. This seems to me, in a certain sense, an expression of the fact that parents, as has been said, are largely absent from the formation of the family. And mothers too are obliged to work outside the home. Communion between them is very fragile. Each family member lives in a world of his or her own: they are isolated in their thoughts and feelings, which are not united. The great problem of this time—in which each person, desiring to have life for himself, loses it because he is isolated and isolates the other from him—is to rediscover the deep communion which in the end can only stem from a foundation that is common to all souls, from the divine presence that unites all of us. I think that the condition for this is to overcome loneliness and misunderstanding, because the latter also results from the fact that thought today is fragmented. Each one seeks his own way of thinking and living and there is no communication in a profound vision of life. Young people feel exposed to new horizons which previous generations do not share; therefore, continuity in the vision of the world is absent, caught up as it is in an ever more rapid succession of new inventions. In ten years changes have taken place which previously never occurred in a hundred years.

> *Meeting with members of the Roman clergy*
> *March 2, 2006*

67. *The demographic winter*

Vast areas of the world are suffering from the so-called "demographic winter," with the consequent gradual ageing of the population. Families sometimes seem ensnared by the fear of life and of parenthood. It is necessary to restore their trust, so that they can continue to carry out their noble mission of procreation in love.

> *Address to participants in the plenary assembly of*
> *the Pontifical Council for the Family*
> *May 13, 2006*

68. *Falling birth rates and precariousness*

There are of course many explanations for the problem of the sharp decline in the birth rate, but certainly a decisive role is also played in this by the fact that people want to enjoy life, that they have little confidence in the future and that they feel the family is no longer viable as a lasting community in which future generations may grow up.

> *Address to the bishops of Switzerland*
> *November 9, 2006*

69. Weak bonds

The great challenge of the new evangelization . . . needs to be sustained with a truly profound reflection on human love, since precisely this love is the privileged path that God chose to reveal himself to man, and in this love he calls human beings to communion in the Trinitarian life. This approach enables us also to overcome a private conception of love that is so widespread today. Authentic love is transformed into a light that guides the whole of life towards its fullness, generating a society in which human beings can live. The communion of life and love which is marriage thus emerges as an authentic good for society. Today, the need to avoid confusing marriage with other types of unions based on weak love is especially urgent. It is only the rock of total, irrevocable love between a man and a woman that can serve as the foundation on which to build a society that will become a home for all mankind.

Address to members of the John Paul II
Institute on Marriage and the Family
May 11, 2006

70. Civil unions

The historical period in which we live asks Christian families to witness with courageous coherence to the fact that procreation is the fruit of love. Such a witness will not fail to encourage politicians and legislators to safeguard the rights of the family. Indeed, it is well known that juridical solutions for the so-called "*de facto*" unions are gaining credibility; although they reject the obligations of marriage, they claim enjoyment of the same rights. Furthermore, at times there are even attempts to give marriage a new definition in order to legalize homosexual unions, attributing to them the right to adopt children.

Address to participants in the plenary assembly of
the Pontifical Council for the Family
May 13, 2006

71. *Licentiousness*

Today, the various forms of the erosion of marriage, such as free unions and "trial marriage," and even pseudo-marriages between people of the same sex, are instead an expression of anarchic freedom that are wrongly made to pass as true human liberation. This pseudo-freedom is based on a trivialization of the body, which inevitably entails the trivialization of the person. Its premise is that the human being can do to himself or herself whatever he or she likes: thus, the body becomes a secondary thing that can be manipulated, from the human point of view, and used as one likes. Licentiousness, which passes for the discovery of the body and its value, is actually a dualism that makes the body despicable, placing it, so to speak, outside the person's authentic being and dignity.

Address to participants in the ecclesial
diocesan convention of Rome
June 6, 2005

72. *Homosexual marriages*

We can . . . see why we do not want some things. I believe we need to see and reflect on the fact that it is not a Catholic invention that man and woman are made for each other so that humanity can go on living: all cultures know this.

Interview before his papal visit to Bavaria
August 5, 2006

73. *Abortion*

As far as abortion is concerned, it is part of the fifth . . . commandment: "You shall not kill!" We have to presume this is obvious and always stress that the human person begins in the mother's womb and remains a human person until his or her last breath. The human person must always be respected as a human person. But all this is clearer if you say it first in a positive way.

Interview before his papal visit to Bavaria
August 5, 2006

74. *Disruptive legislation*

Marriage is becoming, so to speak, ever more marginalized. We are aware of the example of certain countries where legislation has been modified so that marriage is no longer defined as a bond between a man and a woman but a bond between persons; with this, obviously, the basic idea is destroyed and society from its roots becomes something quite different. The awareness that sexuality, *eros* and marriage as a union between a man and a woman go together— "and they become one flesh" (Gn 2:24)—this knowledge is growing weaker and weaker; every type of bond seems entirely normal—they represent a sort of overall morality of non-discrimination and a form of freedom due to man. Naturally, with this the indissolubility of marriage has become almost a utopian idea which many public figures seem precisely to contradict. So it is that even the family is gradually breaking up.

Address to the bishops of Switzerland
November 9, 2006

75. De facto *couples*

At this point, I cannot be silent about my concern about the legislation for *de facto* couples. Many of these couples have chosen this way because—at least for the time being—they do not feel able to accept the legally ordered and binding coexistence of marriage. Thus, they prefer to remain in the simple *de facto* state. When new forms of legislation are created which relativize marriage, the renouncement of the definitive bond obtains, as it were, also a juridical seal. In this case, deciding for those who are already finding it far from easy becomes even more difficult. Then there is in addition, for the other type of couple, the relativization of the difference between the sexes. The union of a man and a woman is being put on a par with the pairing of two people of the same sex, and tacitly confirms those fallacious theories that remove from the human person all the importance of masculinity and femininity, as though it were a question of the purely biological factor. Such theories hold that man—that is, his intellect and his desire—would decide autonomously what he is or what he is not. In this, corporeity is scorned, with the consequence that the human being, in seeking to be emancipated from his body—from the "biological sphere"—ends by destroying himself. If we tell ourselves that the Church ought not to interfere in such matters, we cannot but answer: are we not concerned with the human being? Do not believers, by virtue of the great culture of their faith, have the right to make a pronouncement on all this? Is it not their—our—

duty to raise our voices to defend the human being, that creature who, precisely in the inseparable unity of body and spirit, is the image of God?

Christmas Address to the Roman Curia
December 22, 2006

76. *A painful issue*

A particularly painful situation, as you know, concerns those who are divorced and remarried. The Church, which cannot oppose the will of Christ, firmly maintains the principle of the indissolubility of marriage, while surrounding with the greatest affection those men and women who, for a variety of reasons, fail to respect it. Hence initiatives aimed at blessing irregular unions cannot be admitted.

Address to the French episcopal conference
September 14, 2008

77. The Church's ethical assessment of divorce and abortion

In a cultural context marked by increasing individualism, hedonism and all too often also by a lack of solidarity and adequate social support, human freedom, as it faces life's difficulties, is prompted in its weakness to make decisions that conflict with the indissolubility of the matrimonial bond or with the respect due to human life from the moment of conception, while it is still protected in its mother's womb. Of course, divorce and abortion are decisions of a different kind, which are sometimes made in difficult and dramatic circumstances that are often traumatic and a source of deep suffering for those who make them. They also affect innocent victims: the infant just conceived and not yet born, children involved in the break-up of family ties. These decisions indelibly mark the lives of all those involved. The Church's ethical opinion with regard to divorce and procured abortion is unambivalent and known to all: these are grave sins which, to a different extent and taking into account the evaluation of subjective responsibility, harm the dignity of the human person, involve a profound injustice in human and social relations and offend God himself, Guarantor of the conjugal covenant and the Author of life. Yet the Church, after the example of her Divine Teacher, always has the people themselves before her, especially the weakest and most innocent who are victims of injustice and sin, and also those other men and women who, having perpetrated these acts, stained by sin and wounded within, are seeking peace and the chance to begin anew. The Church's first duty is to approach these people with love and consideration, with caring and motherly attention, to proclaim the merciful closeness of God in Jesus Christ. Indeed, as the Fathers teach, it is he who is the true Good Samaritan, who has made himself close to us, who pours oil and wine on our wounds and takes us into the inn, the Church, where he has us treated, entrusting us to her ministers and personally paying in advance for our recovery. Yes, the Gospel of love and life is also always the *Gospel of mercy*, which is addressed to the actual person and sinner that we are, to help us up after any fall and to recover from any injury.

> *Address to an international gathering organized by*
> *the John Paul II Institute for Marriage and Family*
> *April 5, 2008*

V. THE GOSPEL OF THE FAMILY

78. *The Christian family*

In the Christian vision . . . marriage, which Christ raised to the most exalted dignity of a sacrament, confers greater splendor and depth on the conjugal bond and more powerfully binds the spouses who, blessed by the Lord of the Covenant, promise each other faithfulness until death in love that is open to life. For them, the Lord is the center and heart of the family. He accompanies them in their union and sustains them in their mission to raise children to maturity. In this way the Christian family not only cooperates with God in generating natural life, but also in cultivating the seeds of divine life given in Baptism. These are the well-known principles of the Christian view of marriage and the family.

> *Address to participants in the plenary assembly*
> *of the Pontifical Council for the Family*
> *May 13, 2006*

79. *Difficulties and witnessing*

The family is called to be an "intimate partnership of life and love" (*Gaudium et Spes*, no. 48), because it is founded on indissoluble marriage. Despite the difficulties and the social and cultural conditioning of this period of history, Christian spouses must not cease to be in their lives a sign of God's faithful love: may they collaborate actively with priests in the pastoral guidance of engaged couples, young married couples and families, and in bringing up the new generations.

Address to pilgrims from the Diocese of Verona
June 4, 2005

80. *The model of family*

The spouses' love and total gift of self, with their special connotations of exclusivity, fidelity, permanence in time and openness to life, are at the root of this communion of life and love that constitutes the married state (cf. *Gaudium et Spes*, no. 48). Today, it is necessary to proclaim with renewed enthusiasm that the Gospel of the family is a process of human and spiritual fulfillment in the certainty that the Lord is always present with his grace. This proclamation is often distorted by false concepts of marriage and the family that do not respect God's original plan. In this regard, people have actually reached the point of suggesting new forms of marriage, some unknown to popular cultures in that its specific nature is altered. . . . When such levels are reached, society itself is affected and every kind of risk shakes its foundations.

Address at a meeting on family and
life issues in Latin America
December 3, 2005

81. *The ladder of love*

Christianity, Catholicism, is not a collection of prohibitions: it is a positive option. It is very important that we look at it again because this idea has almost completely disappeared today. We have heard so much about what is not allowed that now it is time to say: we have a positive idea to offer, that man and woman are made for each other, that the scale of sexuality, *eros*, *agape*, indicates the level of love and it is in this way that marriage develops, first of all as a joyful and blessing-filled encounter between a man and a woman, and then, the family, which guarantees continuity among generations and through which generations are reconciled to each other and even cultures can meet.

> *Interview before papal visit to Bavaria*
> *August 5, 2006*

82. *Journey toward maturity*

The joyful love with which our parents welcomed us and accompanied our first steps in this world is like a sacramental sign and prolongation of the benevolent love of God from which we have come. The experience of being welcomed and loved by God and by our parents is always the firm foundation for authentic human growth and authentic development, helping us to mature on the way towards truth and love, and to move beyond ourselves in order to enter into communion with others and with God. To help us advance along the path of human maturity, the Church teaches us to respect and foster the marvelous reality of the indissoluble marriage between man and woman which is also the origin of the family. To recognize and assist this institution is one of the greatest services which can be rendered nowadays to the common good and to the authentic development of individuals and societies, as well as the best means of ensuring the dignity, equality and true freedom of the human person.

Homily at Mass in Valencia, Spain
July 9, 2006

83. *The home of Nazareth*

Children need to be brought up in the faith, to be loved and protected. Along with their basic right to be born and to be raised in the faith, children also have the right to a home which takes as its model the home of Nazareth, and to be shielded from all dangers and threats.

Address at the prayer vigil for the Fifth
World Meeting of Families in Valencia, Spain
July 8, 2006

84. *Domestic Church*

The language of faith is learned in homes where this faith grows and is strengthened through prayer and Christian practice.

Address at the prayer vigil for the Fifth
World Meeting of Families in Valencia, Spain
July 8, 2006

85. *Witness*

The central figure in the work of educating, and especially in education in the faith, which is the summit of the person's formation and is his or her most appropriate horizon, is specifically the form of witness. This witness becomes a proper reference point to the extent that the person can account for the hope that nourishes his life (cf. 1 Pt 3:15) and is personally involved in the truth that he proposes. On the other hand, the witness never refers to himself but to something, or rather, to Someone greater than he, whom he has encountered and whose dependable goodness he has sampled. Thus, every educator and witness finds an unequalled model in Jesus Christ, the Father's great witness, who said nothing about himself but spoke as the Father had taught him (cf. Jn 8:28).

Address to participants in the ecclesial
diocesan convention of Rome
June 6, 2005

86. *Instilling faith*

Faith . . . is not merely a cultural heritage, but the constant working of the grace of God who calls and our human freedom, which can respond or not to his call. Even if no one can answer for another person, Christian parents are still called to give a credible witness of their Christian faith and hope. The need to ensure that God's call and the good news of Christ will reach their children with the utmost clarity and authenticity. As the years pass, this gift of God which the parents have helped set before the eyes of the little ones will also need to be cultivated with wisdom and gentleness, in order to instill in them a capacity for discernment. Thus, with the constant witness of their parents' conjugal love, permeated with a living faith, and with the loving accompaniment of the Christian community, children will be helped better to appropriate the gift of their faith, to discover the deepest meaning of their own lives and to respond with joy and gratitude. The Christian family passes on the faith when parents teach their children to pray and when they pray with them (cf. *Familiaris Consortio*, no. 60); when they lead them to the sacraments and gradually introduce them to the life of the Church; when all join in reading the Bible, letting the light of faith shine on their family life and praising God as our Father.

Homily at Mass in Valencia, Spain
July 9, 2006

87. *Instilling love*

Anyone who knows he is loved is in turn prompted to love. It is the Lord himself, who loved us first, who asks us to place at the center of our lives love for him and for the people he has loved. It is especially adolescents and young people, who feel within them the pressing call to love, who need to be freed from the widespread prejudice that Christianity, with its commandments and prohibitions, sets too many obstacles in the path of the joy of love and, in particular, prevents people from fully enjoying the happiness that men and women find in their love for one another. On the contrary, Christian faith and ethics do not wish to stifle love but to make it healthy, strong and truly free: this is the exact meaning of the Ten Commandments, which are not a series of "no's" but a great "yes" to love and to life.

Address to participants in the ecclesial
diocesan convention of Rome
June 5, 2006

88. *Instilling true freedom*

In contemporary culture, we often see an excessive exaltation of the freedom of the individual as an autonomous subject, as if we were self-created and self-sufficient, apart from our relationship with others and our responsibilities in their regard. Attempts are being made to organize the life of society on the basis of subjective and ephemeral desires alone, with no reference to objective, prior truths such as the dignity of each human being and his inalienable rights and duties, which every social group is called to serve. The Church does not cease to remind us that true human freedom derives from our having been created in God's image and likeness. Christian education is consequently an education in freedom and for freedom. "We do not do good as slaves, who are not free to act otherwise, but we do it because we are personally responsible for the world; because we love truth and goodness, because we love God himself and therefore his creatures as well. This is the true freedom to which the Holy Spirit wants to lead us" (Homily, June 9, 2006). Jesus Christ is the perfect human being, an example of filial freedom, who teaches us to share with others his own love: "As the Father has loved me, so I have loved you; abide in my love" (Jn 15:9).

Homily at Mass in Valencia, Spain
July 9, 2006

89. *Learning the need for crisis*

Today, a crisis point is reached the moment the diversity of temperament is perceived, the difficulty of putting up with each other every day for an entire life. In the end, then, they decided: let us separate. From these testimonies we understood precisely that in crises, in bearing the moment in which it seems that no more can be borne, new doors and a new beauty of love truly open. A beauty consisting of harmony alone is not true beauty. Something is missing, it becomes insufficient. True beauty also needs contrast. Darkness and light complement each other. Even a grape, in order to ripen, does not only need the sun but also the rain, not only the day but also the night. . . . [We] must learn the need for suffering and for crises. We must put up with and transcend this suffering. Only in this way is life enriched. I believe that the fact the Lord bears the stigmata for eternity has a symbolic value. As an expression of the atrocity of suffering and death, today the stigmata are seals of Christ's victory, of the full beauty of his victory and his love for us. We must accept . . . the need to put up with the crises of otherness, of the other, the crisis in which it seems that it is no longer possible to stay together. Husbands and wives must learn to move ahead together, also for love of the children, and thus be newly acquainted with one another, love one another anew with a love far deeper and far truer. So it is that on a long journey, with its suffering, love truly matures.

Meeting with priests of the Diocese of Albano
August 31, 2006

90. *The Gospel of the family*

[We must keep on] proclaiming the Gospel of the family, reaffirming the strength and identity of the family founded upon marriage and open to the generous gift of life, where children are accompanied in their bodily and spiritual growth. This is the best way to counter a widespread hedonism which reduces human relations to banality and empties them of their authentic value and beauty. To promote the values of marriage does not stand in the way of fully experiencing the happiness that man and women encounter in their mutual love. Christian faith and ethics are not meant to stifle love, but to make it healthier, stronger and more truly free. Human love needs to be purified and to mature if it is to be fully human and the principle of a true and lasting joy.

Address at the prayer vigil for the Fifth
World Meeting of Families in Valencia, Spain
July 8, 2006

91. *Message to families*

The Christian family—father, mother and children—is called, then, to do all these things not as a task imposed from without, but rather as a gift of the sacramental grace of marriage poured out upon the spouses. If they remain open to the Spirit and implore his help, he will not fail to bestow on them the love of God the Father made manifest and incarnate in Christ. The presence of the Spirit will help spouses not to lose sight of the source and criterion of their love and self-giving, and to cooperate with him to make it visible and incarnate in every aspect of their lives. The Spirit will also awaken in them a yearning for the definitive encounter with Christ in the house of his Father and our Father. And this is the message of hope that, from Valencia, I wish to share with all the families of the world.

Homily at Mass in Valencia, Spain
July 9, 2006

92. *Christian spouses*

My thoughts now go to all Christian spouses: I thank the Lord with them for the gift of the Sacrament of Marriage, and I urge them to remain faithful to their vocation in every season of life, "in good times and in bad, in sickness and in health," as they promised in the sacramental rite. Conscious of the grace they have received, may Christian husbands and wives build a family open to life and capable of facing united the many complex challenges of our time. Today, there is a special need for their witness. There is a need for families that do not let themselves be swept away by modern cultural currents inspired by hedonism and relativism, and which are ready instead to carry out their mission in the Church and in society with generous dedication.

Angelus
October 8, 2006

93. *The example of Aquila and Priscilla*

This couple [Aquila and Priscilla] in particular demonstrates how important the action of Christian spouses is. When they are supported by the faith and by a strong spirituality, their courageous commitment for the Church and in the Church becomes natural. The daily sharing of their life prolongs and in some way is sublimated in the assuming of a common responsibility in favor of the Mystical Body of Christ, even if just a little part of it. Thus it was in the first generation and thus it will often be. A further lesson we cannot neglect to draw from their example: every home can transform itself into a little church. Not only in the sense that in them must reign the typical Christian love made of altruism and of reciprocal care, but still more in the sense that the whole of family life, based on faith, is called to revolve around the singular lordship of Jesus Christ. Not by chance does Paul compare, in the *Letter to the Ephesians*, the matrimonial relationship to the spousal communion that happens between Christ and the Church (cf. Eph 5:25-33). Even more, we can maintain that the Apostle indirectly models the life of the entire Church on that of the family. And the Church, in reality, is the family of God.

General Audience
February 7, 2007

VI. CHURCH AND FAMILY

94. *The commitment of the Church*

The good that the Church and society as a whole expect from marriage and from the family founded upon marriage is so great as to call for full pastoral commitment to this particular area. Marriage and the family are institutions that must be promoted and defended from every possible misrepresentation of their true nature, since whatever is injurious to them is injurious to society itself.

> *Apostolic Exhortation* The Sacrament of Charity
> (Sacramentum Caritatis), *no. 29*
> *February 22, 2007*

95. *Credible responses*

No man and no woman, however, alone and single-handed, can adequately transmit to children love and the meaning of life. Indeed, to be able to say to someone, "your life is good, even though I may not know your future," requires an authority and credibility superior to what individuals can assume on their own. Christians know that this authority is conferred upon that larger family which God, through his Son Jesus Christ and the gift of the Holy Spirit, created in the story of humanity, that is, upon the Church. Here they recognize the work of that eternal, indestructible love which guarantees permanent meaning to the life of each one of us. . . . For this reason, the edification of each individual Christian family fits into the context of the larger family of the Church, which supports it and carries it with her. . . . And the Church is reciprocally built up by the family, a "small domestic church," as the Second Vatican Council called it (*Lumen Gentium*, no. 11; *Apostolicam Actuositatem*, no. 11), rediscovering an ancient Patristic expression (cf. St. John Chrysostom, *In Genesim Serm.* VI, 2; VII, 1). In the same sense, *Familiaris Consortio* affirms that "Christian marriage . . . constitutes the natural setting in which the human person is introduced into the great family of the Church" (no. 15).

> *Address to participants in the ecclesial
> diocesan convention of Rome
> June 6, 2005*

96. *Learning about family*

One must be re-educated to the desire to know authentic truth, to defend one's own freedom of choice in regard to mass behavior and the lures of propaganda, to nourish passion for moral beauty and a clear conscience. This is the delicate duty of parents and educators who assist them; and it is the duty of the Christian community with regard to its faithful. Concerning the Christian conscience, its growth and nourishment, one cannot be content with fleeting contact with the principal truths of faith in infancy, but a program of accompaniment is necessary along the various stages of life, opening the mind and the heart to welcome the fundamental duties upon which the existence of the individual and the community rest. Only in this way will it be possible to prepare youth to comprehend the values of life, love, marriage and the family. Only in this way can they be brought to appreciate the beauty and the sanctity of the love, joy and responsibility of being parents and collaborators of God in giving life. In the absence of a continuous and qualified formation, the capacity for judgment of the problems posed by biomedicine in the areas of sexuality, newborn life, procreation, and also in the way to treat and care for patients and the weaker sectors of society, becomes even more problematic.

Address to members of the Pontifical Academy for Life
February 24, 2007

97. *The family and the Church*

The family and the Church—in practice, parishes and other forms of Ecclesial Community—are called to collaborate more closely in the fundamental task that consists, inseparably, in the formation of the person and the transmission of the faith. We know well that for an authentic educational endeavor, communicating a correct theory or doctrine does not suffice. Something far greater and more human is needed: the daily experienced closeness that is proper to love, whose most propitious place is above all the family community, but also in a parish, movement or ecclesial association, in which there are people who care for their brothers and sisters because they love them in Christ, particularly children and young people, but also adults, the elderly, the sick and families themselves. The great Patron of educators, St. John Bosco, reminded his spiritual sons that "education is something of the heart and that God alone is its master" (*Epistolario*, 4, 209).

> *Address to participants in the ecclesial*
> *diocesan convention of Rome*
> *June 6, 2005*

98. *The Family of Nazareth*

Prayer, which is personal friendship with Christ and contemplation in him of the face of the Father, is indispensably at the root of the formation of the Christian and of the transmission of the faith. The same is, of course, also true for all our missionary commitment, and particularly for the pastoral care of families: therefore, may the Family of Nazareth be for our families and our communities the object of constant and confident prayer as well as their life model.

*Address to participants in the ecclesial
diocesan convention of Rome
June 6, 2005*

99. *An integral pastoral approach*

It is clear that not only must we seek to get the better of relativism in our work of forming people, but we are also called to counter its destructive predominance in society and culture. Hence, as well as the words of the Church, the witness and public commitment of Christian families is very important, especially in order to reassert the inviolability of human life from conception until its natural end, the unique and irreplaceable value of the family founded on marriage and the need for legislative and administrative measures that support families in the task of bringing children into the world and raising them, an essential duty for our common future. I also offer you my heartfelt thanks for this commitment.

*Address to participants in the ecclesial
diocesan convention of Rome
June 6, 2005*

100. *The family and priestly vocations*

We all know the Church's great need of [vocations to the priesthood and to the consecrated life]! First of all, prayer is crucial in order that these vocations be born and reach maturity, and that those called will always continue to be worthy of their vocation; prayer should never be lacking in any family or Christian community. However, the life witness of priests and men and women religious and their joy in having been called by the Lord are also fundamental. Equally so is the essential example that children receive in their own family and the conviction of families themselves that for them too, the vocation of a child of theirs is a great gift from the Lord. Indeed, the choice of virginity for the love of God and the brethren, which is required for priesthood and for consecrated life, goes hand in hand with the estimation of Christian marriage: both, in two different and complementary ways, make visible in a certain way the mystery of God's Covenant with his people.

Address to participants in the ecclesial
diocesan convention of Rome
June 6, 2005

101. *Spiritual care of families*

The commitment to form strong Christian families proves particularly important to the life of the Church, because the possibility of counting on healthy and generous new generations, as well as of showing them the beauty of a life fully consecrated to Christ and to others, depends precisely on the family. You have therefore rightly made the spiritual care of families the focal point of your efforts, whether those that are newly forming or those that have already been formed and are perhaps experiencing difficulties. The family, which is the fundamental cell of the society on the natural level, is the fundamental school of Christian formation on the supernatural level. The Second Vatican Council rightly presented it as "the domestic church," observing that in it "parents should, by their word and example, be the first preachers of the faith to their children; they should encourage them in the vocation which is proper to each of them, fostering with special care vocations to a sacred state" (*Lumen Gentium*, no. 11).

Address to the bishops of the Czech Republic
on their ad limina *visit*
November 18, 2005

102. *Care of the Christian community toward migrant families*

One must not forget that the family, even the migrant family and the itinerant family, constitutes the original cell of society which must not be destroyed but rather defended with courage and patience. It represents the community in which from infancy the child has been taught to worship and love God, learning the grammar of human and moral values and learning to make good use of freedom in the truth. Unfortunately, in many situations it is difficult for this to happen, especially in the case of those who are caught up in the phenomenon of human mobility. . . . In its action of welcome and dialogue with migrants and itinerant people, the Christian community has, as a constant reference point, the Person of Christ our Lord. He has bequeathed to his disciples a golden rule to abide by in one's own life: the new commandment of love.

> *Address to the Pontifical Council for the Pastoral*
> *Care of Migrants and Itinerant People*
> *May 15, 2008*

103. *Evangelization of the family*

The evangelization of the family is a pastoral priority. . . . The radical changes in contemporary society have broken up numerous families, undermining the family institution with the risk of weakening the very social fabric. It is important at all levels of diocesan and social life to encourage Catholics to preserve and promote the fundamental values of the family. In this spirit, it is right to be attentive to the human and spiritual preparation of couples for marriage and to follow up the pastoral care of families, recalling the eminent dignity of Christian marriage, one and indissoluble, and proposing a solid conjugal spirituality so that families may grow in holiness.

Address to the bishops of the Congo on their ad limina *visit*
February 6, 2006

104. *Family prayer*

Only faith in Christ and only sharing the faith of the Church saves the family; and on the other hand, only if the family is saved can the Church also survive. For the time being, I do not have an effective recipe for this, but it seems to me that we should always bear it in mind. We must therefore do all that favors the family: family circles, family catechesis, and we must teach prayer in the family. This seems to me to be very important: wherever people pray together the Lord makes himself present with that power which can also dissolve "sclerosis" of the heart, that hardness of heart which, according to the Lord, is the real reason for divorce. Nothing else, only the Lord's presence, helps us to truly relive what the Creator wanted at the outset and which the Redeemer renewed. Teach family prayer and thus invite people to pray with the Church and then seek all the other ways.

Meeting with members of the Roman clergy
March 2, 2006

105. *The family of the Church*

Jesus said he was the "Way" that leads to the Father, as well as the "Truth" and the "Life" (cf. Jn 14:5-7). Thus, the question is: how can our children and young people, practically and existentially, find in him this path of salvation and joy? This is precisely the great mission for which the Church exists—as the family of God and the company of friends into which we are already integrated with Baptism as tiny children—in which our faith and joy and the certainty of being loved by the Lord must grow. It is therefore indispensable—and this is the task entrusted to Christian families, priests, catechists and educators, to young people themselves among their peers and to our parishes, associations and movements, and lastly to the entire diocesan community—that the new generations experience the Church as a company of friends who are truly dependable and close in all life's moments and circumstances, whether joyful and gratifying or arduous and obscure; as a company that will never fail us, not even in death, for it carries within it the promise of eternity.

Address to participants in the ecclesial
diocesan convention of Rome
June 5, 2006

106. *Spiritual accompaniment*

The challenges of present-day society, marked by the centrifugal forces generated especially in urban settings, make it necessary to ensure that families do not feel alone. A small family can encounter difficult obstacles when it is isolated from relatives and friends. The ecclesial community therefore has the responsibility of offering support, encouragement and spiritual nourishment which can strengthen the cohesiveness of the family, especially in times of trial or difficulty. Here parishes have an important role to play, as do the various ecclesial associations, called to cooperate as networks of support and a helping hand for the growth of families in faith.

Address at prayer vigil for the
Fifth World Meeting of Families
July 8, 2006

107. *Exchanging gifts*

In so many secularized communities, the first urgent need for believers in Christ is indeed the renewal of the faith of adults so that they can communicate it to the new generations. Moreover, the process of the Christian initiation of children and young people can become a useful opportunity for parents to renew their ties with the Church and learn even more about the beauty and truth of the Gospel. In short, the family is a living organism in which there is a reciprocal exchange of gifts. The important thing is that the Word of God, which keeps the flame of faith alive, never be lacking.

Angelus
July 2, 2006

108. *Sunday*

Dear parents! I ask you to help your children to grow in faith, I ask you to accompany them on their journey towards First Communion, a journey which continues beyond that day, and to keep accompanying them as they make their way to Jesus and with Jesus. Please, go with your children to Church and take part in the Sunday Eucharistic celebration! You will see that this is not time lost; rather, it is the very thing that can keep your family truly united and centered. Sunday becomes more beautiful, the whole week becomes more beautiful, when you go to Sunday Mass together.

Homily at Vespers in Munich, Germany
September 10, 2006

109. *The Holy Family*

In the Gospel we do not find discourses on the family but an *event* which is worth more than any words: God *wanted to be born and to grow up in a human family*. In this way he consecrated the family as the first and ordinary means of his encounter with humanity. In his life spent at Nazareth, Jesus honored the Virgin Mary and the righteous Joseph, remaining under their authority throughout the period of his childhood and his adolescence (cf. Lk 2:41-52). In this way he shed light on the primary value of the family in the education of the person. Jesus was introduced by Mary and Joseph into the religious community and frequented the synagogue of Nazareth. With them, he learned to make the pilgrimage to Jerusalem, as the Gospel passage offered for our meditation by today's liturgy tells us. When he was twelve years old, he stayed behind in the Temple and it took his parents all of three days to find him. With this act he made them understand that he "had to see to his Father's affairs," in other words, to the mission that God had entrusted to him (cf. Lk 2:41-52).

This Gospel episode reveals the most authentic and profound vocation of the family: that is, to accompany each of its members on the path of the discovery of God and of the plan that he has prepared for him or her. Mary and Joseph taught Jesus primarily by their example: in his parents he came to know the full beauty of faith, of love for God and for his Law, as well as the demands of justice, which is totally fulfilled in love (cf. Rom 13:10). From them he learned that it is necessary first of all to do God's will, and that the spiritual bond is worth more than the bond of kinship. The Holy Family of Nazareth is truly the "prototype" of every Christian family which, united in the Sacrament of Marriage and nourished by the Word and the Eucharist, is called to carry out the wonderful vocation and mission of being the living cell not only of society but also of the Church, a sign and instrument of unity for the entire human race.

Angelus
December 31, 2006

110. *The family of the Pope*

Yes, I thank God because I have been able to experience what "family" means; I have been able to experience what "fatherhood" means, so that the words about God as Father were made understandable to me from within; on the basis of human experience, access was opened to me to the great and benevolent Father who is in Heaven. We have a responsibility to him, but at the same time he gives us trust so that the mercy and goodness with which he accepts even our weakness and sustains us may always shine out in his justice, and that we can gradually learn to walk righteously. I thank God for enabling me to have a profound experience of the meaning of motherly goodness, ever open to anyone who seeks shelter and in this very way able to give me freedom. I thank God for my sister and my brother, who with their help have been close to me faithfully throughout my life. I thank God for the companions I have met on my way and for the advisers and friends he has given to me. I am especially grateful to him because, from the very first day of my life, I have been able to enter and to develop in the great community of believers in which the barriers between life and death, between Heaven and earth, are flung open. I give thanks for being able to learn so many things, drawing from the wisdom of this community which not only embraces human experiences from far off times: the wisdom of this community is not only human wisdom; through it, the very wisdom of God—eternal wisdom—reaches us.

Homily at Mass on his eightieth birthday
April 15, 2007

INDEX

(Numbering refers to the sequential positioning of each thought.)

OTHER TITLES *in the Spiritual Thoughts Series*

The Word of God

Draw near to God in an encounter with his word. Pope Benedict XVI breaks open the mystery of the word of God. He explains how receiving the word leads to an encounter with the living word, Jesus Christ. Learn the many dynamic ways God reveals his word to Christians from these selections from Pope's writings, speeches, and sermons.

No. 7-065, 100 pp.

St. Paul

Unite yourselves with Christ! Let Pope Benedict XVI teach you how to share the gift of Christ with the world like St. Paul did. Every page has a thought from the Pope about St. Paul's life and writings. Use the space in the book to record your own thoughts.

No. 7-053, 128 pp.

Mary

Embrace Mary, the Mother of God and all Christians! Pope Benedict XVI shares his thoughts on Mary as the Mother of God in this book. Let the Holy Father's explanation of the special Catholic understanding of Mary's mystery enrich your faith journey.

No. 7-054, 172 pp.

The Saints

Be inspired by Pope Benedict XVI's thoughts about ancient and modern saints. The Holy Father shows how the saints glorified God despite difficulties. Find faith, cling to hope, and learn to love as you read these selections on the saints from the Pope's writings, speeches, and sermons.

No. 7-055, 164 pp.

To order these resources or to obtain a catalog of other USCCB titles, visit *www.usccbpublishing.org* or call toll-free 800-235-8722. In the Washington metropolitan area or from outside the United States, call 202-722-8716. Para pedidos en español, llame al 800-235-8722 y presione 4 para hablar con un representante del servicio al cliente en español.